BLESS THE WEARY

BLESS THE WEARY

Meditations for Congregational Leaders

Edited by **CONNIE GOODBREAD**

Skinner House Books
Boston

Published by Skinner House Books, 24 Farnsworth St., Boston, MA 02210–1409.

skinnerhouse.org

Printed in the United States

Cover design by Alex Camlin
Text design by Tim Holtz

print ISBN: 978-1-55896-988-9
eBook ISBN: 978-1-55896-989-6

5 4 3 2 1
30 29 28 27 26

Cataloging-in-Publication data on file with the Library of Congress.

"Beyond the Zero-Sum Game" from *Exorcising Preaching: Crafting Intellectually Honest Worship* by Nathan C. Walker (Chalice Press, 2014).

"The Church Where Everything Goes Wrong" by Elea Keller from *How We Are Called: A Meditation Anthology*, edited by Mary Benard and Kirstie Anderson (Skinner House Books, 2003).

Excerpt from introduction by Sofía Betancourt in *Love at the Center: Unitarian Universalist Theologies*, edited by Sofía Betancourt (Skinner House Books, 2025).

"God's Work" from *Life Tides* by Elizabeth Tarbox (Skinner House Books, 1993).

"Hope" and "Watching My Friend Pretend Her Heart Isn't Breaking" by Rosemerry Wahtola Trommer from *All the Honey* (Samara Press, 2023), used with permission of the author.

"In a Dangerous Time" by Rosemerry Wahtola Trommer from *A Hundred Falling Veils*, used with permission of the author.

"Litany of 'Oops' and 'Ouch'" from *Incantations for Rest: Poems, Meditations and Other Magic* by Atena O. Danner (Skinner House Books, 2022).

"One Love" by Hope Johnson, "Prayer for Living in Tension" by Joseph M. Cherry, and "We Dream of Peace" by Marta I. Valentín from *Voices from the Margins*, edited by Jacqui James and Mark Morrison-Reed (Skinner House Books, 2012).

"Paddling, No Water" from *Did I Say That Out Loud? Musings from a Questioning Soul* by Meg Barnhouse (Skinner House Books, 2006).

"Pause, Rest, Be" from *Pause, Rest, Be: Stillness Practices for Courage in Times of Change* by Octavia F. Raheem (Shambhala, 2022).

Radical Hospitality by Lonni Collins Pratt and Father Daniel Homan. Copyright 2011. Used by permission of Paraclete Press. paracletepress.com

"Your Very Presence" from *Glory, Hallelujah! Now Please Pick Up Your Socks* by Jane Ellen Mauldin (Skinner House Books, 1998).

Contents

Introduction

Connie Goodbread

> "The job of the church is not to build the church.
> The job of the church is to transform the world."
> —Natalie Briscoe

As I sit down to write this introduction in 2026, the world feels both tender and torn. So much is happening that could distract us, numb us, or convince us that transformation is impossible.

And yet the call to build the world we dream about remains unchanged: a world where every person is supported in becoming all that they can be; where we understand our deep interdependence and know that one person's liberation is bound up with the liberation of all people; where compassion is more common than cruelty, generosity more common than greed.

That dream is still alive—even when it feels distant.

Every generation, I suspect, feels it is living in both the best of times and the worst of times. At this moment, some communities in the United States are experiencing state-sanctioned violence, intimidation, and deep social fracture. It is easy to feel overwhelmed by shock, grief, fear, and anger.

And yet, life continues. The laundry must be done. Children must be fed. The sun rises and sets, painting the sky and water in colors that take our breath away. People reach for one another's hands and lock arms in solidarity. Love persists.

"And I'll bring you hope when hope is hard to find."

Many of us have sung that line in Unitarian Universalist congregations. It raises real questions: What does it mean to bring hope? What does hope look like in seasons of fear? What does it look like in seasons of abundance, when our spirits are steady and the path seems clear?

We are each carrying heavy burdens. We bring them into our relationships, our workplaces, our communities, and our congregations. And we are often searching for the people and spaces that will help us heal. Sometimes we know this; sometimes we do not. As bell hooks reminds us, "Rarely, if ever, are any of us healed in isolation. Healing is an act of communion."

This is true for all of us. It is also true for those who lead, those who serve, and those who hold responsibility—whether in religious communities, families, neighborhoods, or any place where people gather and grow.

Leadership of any kind—professional or volunteer, formal or informal—has never been simple. In calmer times, we still shoulder enormous responsibilities. Add to that natural disasters, global uncertainty, and the everyday challenges of being human, and it becomes clear that all this stress stretches the human spirit.

And yet the human spirit can also be fed—by living courageously, awakening to the wonders of the world, and striving for deeper understanding.

Taking care of ourselves is not indulgence; it is necessity. My friend and colleague Jessica York has often reminded me that we should serve others from the saucer of our overflowing teacup, not from the cup itself.

Yet how often is your cup even full? Depleted people cannot live well. Depleted leaders cannot lead well. Feeding your spirit—resting, laughing, finding joy in ordinary moments—is holy work. Joy in the face of injustice is an act of resistance.

If we can remember who we are, whose we are, and what we value most, then we will come through the struggles of our time whole. We will come through with partners we know well and understand deeply. We will come through with integrity, knowing that we amplified and helped keep sacred our deepest values.

This book is meant to accompany you in remembering who you are, whose you are, and what you value most.

In these pages, you will find reflections that offer grounding when you feel unsteady, companionship when you feel alone, encouragement when your spirit is worn thin, and humor and joy when you need them most. These meditations exist to nourish you—to remind you to rest, to breathe, to reconnect with your purpose, and to trust that transformation happens one choice, one conversation, one act of courage at a time.

May you find hope here.

May these words feed your spirit.

May you find a little humor and a lot of joy.

And when you are restored—even a little—may you go out and, one small act at a time, change the world.

A Blessing for Risk-Takers and Failures

Rev. Robin Tanner

Today we share in a blessing for losers,
risk-takers, all failures far and wide . . .

Blessed are they who fall in the mud,
who jump with gusto and rip their pants,
who skin the elbows and bruise the ego,
for they shall know the sweetness of risk.

Blessed are they who make giant mistakes,
whose intentions are good but whose impact has injured,
who know the hot sense of regret and ask for mercy,
for their hearts will know the gift of forgiveness.

Blessed are they who try again, who dust off,
who wash up, who extend the wish for peace, who
return to sites of failure, who are dogged in their pursuit,
for they will discover the secret to dreams.

Blessed are they who refuse to listen to the naysayers,
for their hearts will be houses for hope.

Blessed are they who see beyond the surface of another,
for they will be able to delight in the gift of compassion.

Blessed are they who stop running the race
to help a fellow traveler, who pick up the fallen,
who stop for injured life,
for they shall know the kindness of strangers.

Blessed are they who wildly, boldly abandon winning,
for they shall know the path of justice.

One More Thing

Rev. Viola Abbitt

In the work
There is always just
One more thing.

One more telephone call
One more visit
One more meeting
One more hand to hold
One more tech problem to solve
One more late night
        and early day
One more . . .

There is always just
One more thing.

And because
there is always just
one more thing,

There is always time for
a walk in sunshine
    or in rain,
laughter with friends,
listening to music and birdsong,
a hug from a loved one,
reading that neglected book,
    and
        whatever else
            you have denied yourself
                for too long.

Include yourself
in the circle of love
in which you place others.

There is always just
one more thing.

Make sure one of them
is to take care of yourself . . .
is for you.

Wishes

Natalie Briscoe

For my Unitarian Universalist siblings,
I have three wishes.

First, I wish for each of you
to have a moment each day
wherein you can
consciously unclench your jaw,
lower your shoulders,
take three deep breaths,
and feel your body
sink into the place
where you can just be.

Second, I wish for each of you
a community, be it one or
one hundred, that
recognizes the
squeak in your voice that
means the sparrow of

trauma is caught in
your throat again.
And I want them to say
yes, it does hurt,
and I will be here while
you cough yourself clear,
until it comes scratching up
your throat like truth
and feathers.

And finally, I wish for each of you
the freedom to feel
whatever you feel.
To cry whenever you need,
for however long you need.
To laugh whenever you need,
for however long you need,
or to do both at the same time,
accepting the fullness of your
mind and heart as it crashes
through you like waves,
free of any judgment
from yourself or others.

And in this way,
I wish for you
extravagant, faithful
unbounded Love.

From *Pause, Rest, Be*

Octavia F. Raheem

Listen. We are descending into quiet. Being thrown into it, really. I hear a sound so striking in its silence that it has displaced us all. It has put us in our place.

Human.

Be. Still.

We can no longer outrun this without collectively slowing down. We cannot profit from this without the bottom meticulously falling out. We cannot package, sell, or otherwise capitalize on this without paying with our very own lives.

We can no longer live in the way that so many of us have learned to be:

Individual

Grinding

Hustling

Calculating

Competitive

Consumed with work

Away from our families while saying . . . family matters.

We cannot outrun this. The only way to beat this is to stop. Now. And still, some of us may lose.

There can be no screaming match here. If we keep yelling over everything and everybody, we will miss it.

So, stop. Really, stop. Go read. write. rest. take care. paint. cry. dance. love. sit in the rain. grieve. reconnect to the source of your strength. cook at home. call your elders. pray. love. be transformed.

In a Dangerous Time

Rosemerry Wahtola Trommer

I think of the bones
of the unsung rib cage,
the way they protect
the heart. How bone,
too, is living, how it constantly
renews and remakes itself.
I think of how ribs engage
with other ribs
to expand, to contract,
and because they do
their solid work,
they allow the heart to float.
This is what I want to do:
to be a rib in this body
of our country,
to make a safe space for love.
There is so much now
that needs protection.

I want to be that flexible,
that committed to what's vital,
that unwilling to yield.

"Don't Worry About It" (Said No Helpful Advice Ever)

Rev. Nathan Detering

Worship was starting in fifteen minutes. I should have been out in the front of the sanctuary greeting people as they came in, something I have done over my entire ministry. Instead, I was in my office with the door closed, gripping the edges of my desk so hard that my fingers turned white.

"*Nathan, what's wrong with you?*" I said to myself. "*Just chill!*"

I didn't have the language for it then, but I was in the midst of a full-on panic attack. Room spinning, cold sweat on the back of my neck, trembling hands. Only weeks earlier I had been halfway across the country standing at the graveside of my dad, who had died suddenly only two years after my younger brother died of a drug overdose. My family and I had been through the wringer.

When congregants suffer losses like these, I tell them to take the time they need to feel all their feelings, but I have a much harder time showing myself the same grace. Instead, I tell myself not to worry about it and push on. Isn't that what being a minister for others demands?

I somehow made it through worship that day, but I shouldn't have even tried. What I should have done is ask for help, and in doing so testified against the white supremacy culture that prizes performance and perfection over vulnerability and authenticity.

It was my spouse, who loves me enough to tell the things I don't want to hear, who said it was time I needed to ask for help. When I told her not to worry about it, "I'm fine," she persisted.

But when the next day came and the panic was still there, I relented. My body was telling me that I hadn't taken the time to properly grieve my dad or my brother before launching back into life and work. So I called the therapist I had let slide years ago because I thought I was "fine," who encouraged me to do the thing that feels so easy to preach about but so hard for me to practice: I told my family, my friends, and my close colleagues that

I was suffering from anxiety. To my shock and relief, no one told me, "Don't worry about it!" Instead, they listened, and they loved.

Then, after months of counseling, acquiring tools to help with my anxiety, and grieving the losses I hadn't grieved, I did the next hard thing. I told the congregation. I told them about my panic attacks, the unresolved grief, the harm that comes from the culture that tells us we have to perform perfectly instead of taking the time we need to get the care we need. I thought I could get through that sermon without the tears coming, but when I saw them in others, I knew we could be honest together.

I ended by saying this:

> Let's help each other breathe.
> Don't pretend.
> Exhale. Talk about your fears and your hopes.
> Exhale. Breathe. Inspire. Draw in breath here.
> Don't pretend.
> When you're anxious, tell someone. When you're depressed, call us.

Community can't fix everything; nothing can fix
everything.
But surely, we're part of what can help.
You have done that for me. Let this community
do that for you.

It wasn't the best sermon I have ever given, but many told me it was maybe the most important. Sometimes we preach the sermon we most need to hear, and sometimes what we need to hear is what others need too.

The Minister (Who I Am)

Rev. Linda Hart

My identity as a minister is
painted on my throat:
the small piece of plastic,
tucked into the collar of
my black shirt,
a Rorschach test for
all the wounds
that strangers carry in the
part of their psyche
called "religion."

Sometimes I want
to cover myself
with patches and stickers
like race car drivers:
a rainbow flag
on my right shoulder,
"prays well with others"

pressed into a heart shape
just over my left breast,
a "Namaste, Motherfucker"
bumper sticker applied
on my lower back.

Maybe I should
adorn myself more:
a teardrop inked
under my left eye,
since heartbreak
and grief always abide;
"faith" and "doubt"
etched into my palms,
so that when I clasp my hands
the two kiss.

I am petty too often,
judging too harshly,
that gaze turned on
me as much as others,
maybe more.
I can't be righteous
as a tent revival preacher,

offering condemnation
and a false salvation.

Instead, I try to point
toward beauty
that can save:
the scarlet leaves
lit perfectly by the
sun slipping to the horizon;
the face of a grocery
clerk when he laughs
at a joke;
the sweetness of tears
of grief, love wet on
your face.

Sustainably Working Toward Collective Liberation

Diane Melvin

"What is the antidote to exhaustion?" poet David Whyte asked Brother David Steindle-Rast.

To which he replied, "The antidote to exhaustion is wholehearted presence."

Feeling tired and overwhelmed day after day is such a painful way to live. Deeply indoctrinated messages about the Protestant work ethic combined with my own wounds around inadequacy created the perfect conditions for spending most of my life "hustling for my worth." Feeling valued when people recognized and appreciated the outcomes of my hard work, I strove for decades to build and nurture a large and vibrant religious education program in my congregation. But the price of years of overworking at an unsustainable pace has come due.

I crossed over the threshold into my sabbatical leave feeling completely exhausted and burned out. It took six weeks of daily spiritual and somatic practices before my nervous system began to let down. I embarked upon a path of deep healing, consciously rooting out the places within me that held onto false correlations between my productivity and my worth. I wanted to weed out the messages that falsely proclaimed I am "not good enough" or "too much." I worked to decolonize myself from fostering the white supremacist values of individualism, perfectionism, urgency, and efficiency at all cost.

"Grind culture is a collaboration between white supremacy and capitalism. It views our divine bodies as machines. Our worth is not connected to how much we produce," declares Tricia Hersey in her manifesto *Rest Is Resistance.*

Hersey's wisdom helped me to recognize how I perpetuate white supremacy culture when I consistently work to the point of overwhelm and exhaustion. I have ignored the exhaustion in my body in order to work at the pace I felt was expected of me. My inner driver is relentless, and the cost of adherence has accumulated over time to manifest in diminished physical, mental, and spiritual health.

I am trying to practice fierce and tender self-compassion as an antidote to my inner critic. Instead of continued self-flagellation and pushing through, I'm learning to listen within and compassionately heed my body's limits and wisdom. By slowing down my frenetic pace and actually stopping when I am tired, I hope to unravel these false and harmful narratives and habits from deep within myself.

As Atena O. Danner elegantly states in her poem "A Spell for Warriors and Heroes," "Together we grow toward liberation at the speed of care." I try to imagine what the speed of care looks like. I suspect that if it is to be truly inclusive, it may be quite slow. Slowing down not only creates more ease for my own body and spirit; it is also a subversive act to resist and dismantle grind culture, hopefully creating more ease for all who come after me as well.

More important than the quantity of things I accomplish is the spirit with which I approach them. Am I rushing from one thing to the next, trying to do all the things? Or am I bringing a grounded and wholehearted presence?

How can we work and live out our UU values from a well-rested place of wholeness and balance? How can we resist the siren calls of always striving to do more and do it faster? How do we check ourselves with our outsized expectations of staff and volunteers in our congregations?

While our work is important, learning how to do it sustainably is an integral part of the work. May we find creative ways to disengage from and dismantle grind culture as we work to build the Beloved Community with collective liberation for all beings.

Beyond the Zero-Sum Game

Rev. Nathan C. Walker, *Exorcising Preaching*

For centuries, insiders
have been democratizing their religions.

Incremental moments of institutional reform
have led to a new era of theological enlightenment.

From out of ancient times
into the twilight of now,
these reformers have made a sacred vow:
to never mischaracterize freedom
as a zero-sum game.

True freedom is not jealous.
True freedom is not envious.
True freedom is not spiteful.

True freedom does not desire
to restrict the rights of others.
True freedom knows not a selfish thought,
knows not how to threaten.

To sense true freedom is to know that
your win is my glory and that
your suffering is inextricably tied to my own.

For the sum of all that is holy shines far beyond
the tools of our evolving democracy—
from party jingles to picket signs.

The sum of all that is holy is found
In our collective desire to know freedom
not as a political slogan,
but as a way of life.

Unbreakable Connections

Rev. Daniel Lawlor

Let us recall Rev. Dr. Howard Thurman's invitation, "Keep open the heart."

Our Unitarian and Universalist religious traditions—religious movements for spiritual exploration and organized compassion—were born and grew during times of war.

Throughout our history, tens of thousands of lay leaders and ministers have proclaimed love and the necessity of a wider circle of care within the context of religious bigotry, white supremacy, gendered violence, and social inequality. This has been true whether in nineteenth-century North American cities, where determined communities struggled against the brutal enslaver elite both within and without their congregations; in twentieth-century communities across the Pacific, from Universalists in Daegu and Manila to Unitarians in Honolulu, striving for human rights in the aftermath of

World War II; or in twenty-first-century North American communities proclaiming love in the shadows of mass incarceration, violence, and Covid-19.

In each generation, the wider conflicts between democracy or autocracy have shaped the choices we have made to resist, create alternatives to, avoid, be complicit with, or actively support freedom or repression. May we learn from the inspirations, ambiguities, and failings of our past as we respond to the present and build for the future.

Unitarian, Universalist, and Unitarian Universalist traditions are embodied in progressive religious communities around the world, from the Philippines to South Africa. In the United States, we are called to embody love in places that are haunted by the ghosts of Jim Crow. To do this work, we must exorcize the spirits of violence, race, and class exclusion that haunt our congregations. We must repent of past harms as we build a twenty-first-century Unitarian Universalism of sustaining and growing love.

Wherever we are, we affirm there are multiple paths to Spirit and goodness, and we invite each other to build sustainable efforts of compassion. From proclaiming trans lives are divine to organizing mutual aid, from working for just, inclusive communities to visiting the sick, from meditating and singing by the chalice to being in solidarity with families in mourning, we are called to gather and act, to restore our spirits and repair our world.

Unitarian Universalists affirm that all life is unbreakably connected. We say local religious communities can organize, care for one another and choose their own leaders; that ministers have the responsibility and freedom of the pulpit and individuals have the responsibility and freedom of conscience. We also find sacred scriptures that point toward compassion in varied works of inspiration and in the natural world.

An ancestor in our tradition, Miguel Servetus, a sixteenth-century physician from Spain who was killed for advocating for wider religious freedom, once wrote, "Ardua magis res est amare, quam credere:" it is harder to love than to believe. For centuries in our tradition, acts of love have been more valued than any particular words or phrases about love. Showing up—actually being present—is harder than saying one will be present. Which makes those moments of connection all the more special.

I don't know about you, but I'm happy and humbled to be part of a tradition of love-seeking religious communities. At their best, our ancestors remind us that we are all tied together, that the Sacred is all around us, and that we have obligations to one another.

The Prophet Isaiah once implored those seeking the Holy to sustain a "house of prayer for all people." And the truth is, I need that reminder because now is a heartache time.

Thank you for your and your communities' practices of faith, especially now. May we hear and respond to the invitation to be open to this aching world and grow in love and repair together.

Naming Things Out Loud

Rev. Erika Hewitt

My friend and I were chatting on the phone on a Tuesday morning when our conversation veered off-course.

"There's a truck at the curb," Beth narrated, "and someone's walking up to my door." A captive audience, I listened to the visitor—Dan—introduce himself. He'd received a call about leaky gutters, he said. Did Beth want him to take a look now or return later?

I heard Beth pause and then reply, clear as a bell, "I have penguins on my pajamas."

This is why I love my friend so much: for her, it comes naturally to disarm awkwardness by naming the figurative elephant (and the literal penguins) in the room. While I can only imagine the look on Dan's face as he processed Beth's ensemble, I admired her forthrightness when most of us would have just stewed in discomfort.

Maybe I could practice that, I thought to myself.

It's not just that I too have been caught in my jammies at an hour when most people are subject to a workplace dress code (although I have). I'm someone who tends to freeze up when things feel awkward or messy—especially when I think I've contributed to the mess. In my moments of freezing up, I can feel my lizard brain go into contortions—by which I mean I feel an overwhelming urge to flee into the kitchen and eat ice cream straight from the container.

It took me years to realize that many uncomfortable conversations go better when I'm brave enough to name the source of tension. But sometimes I forget that this is a practice; that like all practices, it grows easier the more you do it.

A few weeks later, my supervisor met with me and presented a complicated new system for tracking my work projects. I felt a familiar stirring—*Lo! The lizard has awoken while the rest of me is freezing up*—when an inner voice finally prompted me: *This is your chance to say something about the penguins.*

I cleared my throat. "I'm feeling anxious and defensive,"

I ventured, "because I'm wondering if this new system means that you've been unhappy with my follow-through on projects."

My supervisor explained, kindly, that she had no concerns about my work; she was trying to learn and implement new skills as a manager. We were trying something new together. And I returned, fully present, to our conversation. (I also came to love the new system!)

The most beautiful thing about naming what's so—whether it's "I'm wearing pajamas in front of the gutter guy" or "I'm worried that you're unhappy with me"—is that it also helps us practice naming bigger, more important truths. Ones like "I don't think racist jokes are funny" or "Our relationship has taken a hit, and I wonder if we could begin to repair it."

What we practice grows stronger. What we practice grows more graceful. May we all be brave enough to name our truths, each a shining gem, as we offer those truths to one another.

Litany of Oops and Ouch

ATENA O. DANNER, *Incantations for Rest*

I receive your "Ouch" with openness and curiosity.
    I receive your "Oops" with acceptance and empathy.
I offer my "Ouch" with hope and trust.
    I offer my "Oops" with humility and courage.
I release my "Ouch" with immeasurable faith.
    I release my "Oops" with purpose.
I release your "Ouch" with promise.
    I release your "Oops" with my eyes and heart open.

Holy Interruption

Rev. Julica Hermann de la Fuente

> "There's no such thing as neutral education. Education either functions as an instrument to bring about conformity or freedom."
>
> —Paulo Freire, *Pedagogy of the Oppressed*

One of the most humbling lessons of my antiracism education career was when I witnessed a difficult and racist presentation in a Unitarian Universalist gathering, and I didn't think it was mine to interrupt. In fact, there were over forty people in the room, and nobody thought it was theirs to interrupt. It was like witnessing a train wreck in slow motion. It was terrible. And no one said "stop."

When the speaker was finished, we all struggled to process what had just happened. No one said, "We need a caucus for the people of color in the room"—because there were six of us—"to figure out what we need." There was stark silence, followed by tortured conversation.

I learned that day that if I am in the room, it's my responsibility to interrupt when someone is being harmed, and to center their (our) needs. It doesn't matter what my hierarchical position is in the system; I'm part of a covenantal community and when a covenant gets broken, it's my responsibility to name that break, with kindness and the intention of healing, and to call us back into right relationship.

To throw a wrench into the agenda is one of the more destabilizing things that we can do in majority-white spaces, because white supremacy culture teaches us to be efficient, to stay on task, to aim for perfection. The alternative is being relational; instead of staying on task, we can pay attention to what just happened and what needs to be done in order to restore right relationship. We can center those who have been placed at the margins.

This holy muscle of interruption is about courage, about a commitment to love at a higher level, about liberation and wholeness. It's about being willing to risk being unpopular in the moment and taking the heat that will happen when you interrupt the process.

When something happens that requires interrupting, it's ours to do—and the more privilege we have according to our social location, the more responsibility we have to leverage that privilege. When we do, we bring the beloved community into being in that moment.

Queridisma Diosa: help us strengthen our muscles to interrupt in love. Help us honor relationships and lived experiences in real time, centering the needs of those that have been harmed and restoring what has been broken. Bendita Seas, amén.

Steadfast in This Faith

Rev. Naftali King

We are called to this church to use our hearts and hands and minds to bring hope to each other. . . . We are first and foremost listening to where our hearts are calling us, checking out that call with our minds, and putting our bodies to work.

Knowing where we are called and to what meaningful work and to which relationships is an amazing, life-affirming gift. It would be an amazing experience and great gift if these calls happened only once in our lives. But even more generously, even more amazingly, they don't just happen once, but repeatedly, every time we're tested and every time something about us changes. . . .

What we do here extends beyond these doors, throughout everything we do and touch in our entire lives. We're doing church even when we're not at church. We're doing church the other six days of the week. We're doing church everywhere we go, every moment. We are making the choice constantly to be steadfast in this faith and to make hope real.

Your Very Presence

REV. DR. JANE ELLEN MAULDIN, *Glory, Hallelujah*

A number of years ago my brother lay dying in the hospital. He spent days in the intensive care unit while members of the family, including my mother, sat for many long hours on chairs in the hallway outside his room. Among the visitors who came to share the vigil was a member of our church.

How are you doing? the friend asked.

My mother was too exhausted to tell anything but the truth. *I'm tired*, she said. *I'm very, very tired. I'm too tired to even pray any more.*

But don't you see, her friend replied, *your very presence is a prayer.*

There are times when all words fail us, all forms seem hollow, and no one out there or inside seems to be listening. At those times, our presence, just our presence, is prayer. Our bodies, our actions, become our prayer, our connection to God, whatever God may be.

From *Love at the Center*

Rev. Dr. Sofía Betancourt

Unitarian Universalists have long understood ourselves to be bearers of love and justice in the world—those who show up for peace and freedom, who side with love in the face of all that would otherwise diminish our humanity.

Love is what we express as our highest value. Every time. Larger than life. Right at the center of our living tradition. Our pressing task now is to ask ourselves and each other how this understanding calls us forward, individually and collectively. We may agree that love is central, but what does that mean to us and what does it require of us?

The love that lives at the center of this faith is a love that expects nothing less of us than the rebuilding of this struggling world. Sometimes what we know of love and justice pushes us in ways we never expected. And sometimes the need to bear such love into the world is heartbreakingly large. It is in those moments that we most need one another, and most need beloved community. We need reminding and solidarity, connection and care. Our freely made choice to participate in that greater community can slowly renew us and even repair the kinds of grief that have been building for many of us, to restore what we long to hold at our own centers and to heal that which keeps us from being more loving.

It takes many of us, in community, to insist that a better future is possible, to keep us faithful to our commitments when we err or falter, and to remind us that we are constantly connected to a hope-filled belief in human goodness and capacity for love, even when we feel furthest from that which is larger than our own knowing.

Given everything our world faces today, having faith in love is no small thing.

Watching My Friend Pretend Her Heart Isn't Breaking

ROSEMERRY WAHTOLA TROMMER, *All the Honey*

On Earth, just a teaspoon of neutron star
would weigh six billion tons. Six billion tons
equals the collective weight of every animal
on earth. Including the insects. Times three.

Six billion tons sounds impossible
until I consider how it is to swallow grief—
just a teaspoon and one might as well have consumed
a neutron star. How dense it is,
how it carries inside it the memory of collapse.
How difficult it is to move then.
How impossible to believe that anything
could lift that weight.

There are many reasons to treat each other
with great tenderness. One is
the sheer miracle that we are here together

on a planet surrounded by dying stars.
One is that we cannot see what
anyone else has swallowed.

Prayers for the Brave and Burdened

Rev. Derail Holcomb

Divine Spirit, Source of love and compassion,

Today we are seeking solace and strength for those who tirelessly serve our congregations and faith, feeling burned out and discouraged. We hold in our hearts those of all ages who, with unwavering dedication, strive to amplify the values at the heart of Unitarian Universalism. They are our partners on this sacred journey, and today we lift them up in love, strength, power, and prayer.

In this interconnected web of existence, we recognize that our community is woven together by the threads of diverse perspectives, shared struggles, and a deep desire to nurture love and justice in the world. We acknowledge the immense challenges faced by those who lead the way, and who carry the weight of our collective aspirations. May they find solace in knowing that they are not alone in their struggles.

Grant them, O Divine, the strength to persevere when the road seems steep and the way forward uncertain. Shower them with reassurance when doubts and weariness threaten their spirits. May they find partners in fellow seekers who share their dedication and offer unwavering support. Let them discover nourishment for their souls in embracing a community that cherishes their presence.

In this journey of faith, we celebrate imperfection as a permission-giving path toward growth and transformation. Help us cultivate a community where vulnerability is seen as a strength and where the wisdom of shared experience nourishes our collective understanding. May we extend grace and kindness to those who stumble, knowing that true growth and learning can occur through these humbling moments.

Light! Guide our souls. Help us to create spaces where leadership is seen as an invitation to vulnerability, authenticity, and trust. May our congregations and faith communities be sanctuaries offering respite, understanding, and renewal for those who diligently work to bring about a more just and compassionate world. Let us be steadfast in our commitment to fostering a culture of support, where burdens are shared and joys are multiplied.

As we send forth this prayer, may it be a beacon of hope for all who serve, reminding them that their efforts are seen and cherished. May it kindle within them a renewed sense of purpose and remind them that they are held in the loving embrace of a compassionate community.

With gratitude and humility, we offer this meditation, trusting that love will prevail and that together, we shall continue to walk humbly with one another. Ashé.

Let Beauty In

Rev. Dr. Rebekah Savage

Let beauty in.
Let beauty in like waves lapping on the shore,
covering the beach and soaking the sand like an embrace.

Let beauty in.
Let beauty in like the first sunshine after a cloudy day,
filling hearts and homes with a radiance that brings delight.

Let beauty in.
Let beauty in like a wrapped gift from the Spirit of
Life herself, as She offers to us:
"Behold what creation can do.
Behold, this is love made real that you can touch, taste,
and smell all around you."

May all that is pleasing and exquisite be nurtured here
in our time of worship.
May the magnificent pull towards all that is divinely
pleasing hold us close.
May the Sacred pulse within this space as we welcome
in Beauty.

Anchored by Hope

Rev. Dr. Oscar Sinclair

> "[Hope] transcends the world that is immediately experienced, and is anchored somewhere beyond its horizons. Hope . . . is not the same as joy that things are going well . . . but, rather, an ability to work for something because it is good, not just because it stands a chance to succeed."
>
> —Vaclav Havel

My apartment looks out on the Mississippi River, where I watch barges travel back and forth each morning. But on nights when I wake up after midnight, scared and uncertain about what the months and years ahead will hold, I find my mind drifting from river barges back to my adopted hometown of Baltimore, of oceans and sailing ships.

Usually I think of anchors as something to keep us in place, to hold us steady as the world around us moves.

But there's at least one other use for an anchor. Imagine an old sailing ship: on a big, 150-foot schooner, there aren't any motors or oars on the boat itself. The ship is designed to work with the wind; when you're out in the open sea with the wind at your back, it cuts through the waves fast and straight.

But how does the ship get out of port? What do you do when the wind isn't at your back, but coming straight at your face? Maybe you're stuck, no wind to be had at all.

There's at least one other way to use an anchor, called warping. The crew of a becalmed ship would take a kedge anchor and put it in a rowboat. A crew rowed it as far as they could out in front of the ship and dropped the anchor. The crew aboard the ship hauled on the anchor—not bringing it up, but bringing the ship slowly overtop of the anchor. Then they pulled the anchor up, put it back on the rowboat, and repeated the process. It's not fast, and it takes an enormous amount of work from many people working together, but in this way even the largest sailing ship can move forward without any wind.

I think of an anchor as a kind of motivation when the wind is against us. Hope doesn't require that the wind be at our backs; it's not moored to a certain understanding of the experienced world. Hope is challenging, if not impossible, to grasp alone. Hope, in this sense, is a discipline to anchor myself to something that I can't quite grasp yet, but I trust is there—and a discipline to pull towards that goal together, one day at a time.

Prayer

God of all that is spoken and all held too close to be said aloud, help us to hold on to hope. When we find ourselves becalmed, remind us to drop an anchor over the horizon; pull along with us as we haul toward a more hopeful horizon.

Reflection During Frustrating Times

Pastor Joshua Berg

We are frustrated.

With struggle.
With the cycle of struggle and relief
And struggle again.
With the knowledge that struggle is a part of life.

We hope for the continued awareness
That struggle builds resistance,
That struggle increases strength.
That the cycle includes
Relief between struggles
And relief yet again
Also, always, a part of life.

We are frustrated.

With confusion
With not knowing
With knowing what we should not
With knowing
What we do not want to know

We hope for knowledge
Of what is helpful
Of what is healing
Of what is uplifting and empowering
Of what inspires us to compassion
Of what helps us
To know each other as ourselves.

We are frustrated.

With waiting
With wanting
With needing
With worrying.

We hope for
Hearing, smelling, seeing, touching, feeling,
And sensing
Others with grace.

We hope for sharing.
We hope for love.
We hope for being
What we need to be
That frustration may cease.

We are frustrated.

We hope that naming our frustration—
Calling it out powerfully
In this moment—
Makes it easier to meet the next.

The Long Game

Rev. Shari Woodbury

> "Can you coax your mind from its wandering
> and keep to the original oneness?
> Can you let your body become supple as a newborn child's?
> Can you deal with the most vital matters by letting events take their course?
> Can you step back from your own mind and thus understand all things?"
>
> —Tao te Ching
> (Stephen Mitchell translation)

The longest winter of my life took place while I was in congregational leadership. I needed respite from the challenges of that work: policy decisions that were sure to displease some of the people all of the time, a struggle to keep enough volunteers involved to maintain the most basic functions of church, the adaptive imperative of finding new ways to connect our members and welcome visitors.

In that discouraging era to be in leadership, the growing dark of winter sometimes seemed a mirror for my inner landscape. I knew that this winter in church life would eventually turn to spring, even if the timing might be less predictable than nature's. But how could I cope in the meantime and continue to give my best as a leader?

When I needed a break, I headed to the ping-pong table in the basement. Keeping my eye on a bouncing ball was better than getting lost in a stream of gloomy news coverage or going down social media rabbit holes. When I had a red paddle in my hand, my mind returned to a single point; my body nimbly took over.

My spouse and I have been playing ping-pong for over a decade, since we first started dating. We are well-matched players. But something new happened during that winter marathon: we each had rather long winning streaks. Why?

When I reigned over the green table, it was largely because I was leaning into my strengths, so deliberate in my placement of the ball. Lobbing plenty of them right on the edge of the table. Making him run all over, breathless, to return my hits. Sneaking in a short shot after he'd stepped back to return a long one.

My husband had a very different approach. He was constantly experimenting with his technique: a tricky spin, a high-velocity serve, reinvention of his strokes every couple of weeks. He wanted to keep our tournament engrossing until the crocuses were finally popping up—and he did. We made it through that long winter and its trying events.

Vital matters continue to unfold at their own pace, testing my patience and my leadership skills from time to time. As I face today's challenges, I want to remember what enabled our ping-pong breakthroughs: making the most of our strengths and embracing the risks of experimentation. If all else fails, I want to remember to get out of my worrying mind and back into my body.

Prayer

Original Oneness, draw me back to you. When I am knotted and scattered, coax me back to primordial connectedness with All That Is. Help me to find my singular, supple place among the ten thousand things.

Imperfect Human Beings

REV. DEANNA VANDIVER

Sometimes my partner and I like to play a game called Boggle. It is a pretty simple set up—a square filled with dice with letters on them and a lid that lets you shake them up. To play, set a timer and begin to find as many words as you can from the letters that touch. Scoring is a matter of reading your list to the other person. Any word that you both found gets crossed off both your lists and you get points for the words only you found.

It was in playing Boggle together that we began to fully appreciate how very differently we perceive the world. Once we each got eight points with *no* words crossed off either of our lists. This means we both looked at the same square of letters for two minutes and saw completely different words. It was little mind-boggling, in truth. And it served as a powerful spiritual practice for appreciating how much of the world I would miss without my partner's perspective.

As I live into the complexities of working for our collective well-being within faith institutions, I am grateful for this reminder that I cannot perceive all the possibilities by myself. We need each other to co-create Beloved Community. It is only in relationship that the world opens more fully, that love and liberation can truly unfold.

Spirit of life and love, may I remember that my way is only one way of perceiving the world. It takes all of us to get free together. May I practice collaborative leadership with curiosity, compassion, and gratitude for what becomes possible when we create in community.

Puzzling Our Way Through

Rev. Emily Gage

For about two years now, we have had a jigsaw puzzle table up and running at our house. We started when my wife had surgery, and as that limited her pickleball hobby at the time, she turned to puzzles. Right after that I had surgery, and then suddenly we were in a pandemic and we never took the puzzle table down. We have been through scores and scores of puzzles, mostly of 1000 pieces. You name it, we have probably done a puzzle of it.

While different puzzles require different strategies, we generally start by sorting out the edge pieces and putting them together before anything else. It helps me to get a better sense of what we are dealing with—the size and scope of the puzzle. From there we just see what grabs our attention and follow it accordingly. Sometimes the images are clear and easy to follow and the pieces vary in size and shape, and sometimes every piece looks exactly alike. Sometimes moving forward requires that you try every single piece until a fit is found. It can be tedious.

I guess it goes without saying that I love puzzles because I appreciate a concrete set of challenges. I like the way my mind gets occupied in a way that feels meditative. I love the sense of accomplishment when a long looked-for piece appears. Having a puzzle to focus on has felt like a way to alleviate some of the stress of pandemic life.

We are currently working on a puzzle with so many different colors and images and piece shapes that we decided to do it without looking at the final picture to know where we are going. (Perhaps fittingly, it depicts mystery novels.) I'm enjoying the extra challenge, and it makes the puzzle completion a whole different experience. Instead of comparing a piece to the larger picture to figure out where it fits in, you can only look at the pieces and see where they fit together, one or a few at a time, not knowing where they will lead. Slowly but surely, the big picture and final product emerge.

You know, kind of like life these days. Or maybe always.

This December, again, we are figuring out things in new ways, affected by the ever-evolving conditions of the pandemic. In our congregation, we are processing our past and letting go to build a new future. In our lives, we are renegotiating what we can count on and what we can't as we figure out new ways to be and do. One piece at a time, trying them all until they connect with another piece, and so on and so forth.

As I write, I'm sitting right next to the table with the unfinished mystery novel puzzle. Some things have been connected to the framework, but mostly, it's a bunch of unconnected chunks of pieces looking for a place to fit. Still, I'm not worried. I know we'll keep on working and figure it all out; we always do. Thank goodness we are all in this together, bringing our own perspectives and wisdom to bring the big picture into view.

Beautiful Chaos

Connie Goodbread

Beautiful Chaos
Arrived with boxes and luggage and pets and bags.
Arrived in a whirlwind of laughter and plans and
uncertain futures.
Arrived to stay for hours, days, and months.
Arrived.

Beautiful Chaos
Stayed and turned everything upside down.
Stayed and made piles of clothes and books and dog
hair and leftovers.
Stayed and made plans fall apart and need to be rethought.
Stayed.

Beautiful Chaos
Left and took some boxes and luggage and pets and bags.
Left and calm took over, the to-do list and the "where
were we" remembered.
Left and took a bit of my heart with it as it drove away.

Left.

Beautiful Chaos

Don't think you are not welcome or that the mess is
too much.

I love you more than you will ever know.

Each and every little part of you.

Come home when you can.

How to Do This

Rev. Victoria Safford

It is more than we are built to hold:
the cruelty
the damage
the danger that seeps now under every threshold,
sometimes breaking down the door.

It is more than we are built to hold:
the grief
the strange shame lurking in the shadow of the mind,
whispering that we could, we should, do more to resist
(but honestly we don't know what),
the rage with nowhere to go.

It is more than we are built to hold
in our bodies, in our bones,
and it's just beginning
and already we are weary beyond words.

But
consider the elephants.
In the zoo in San Diego, they felt in their giant, quiet feet
the tremors of an earthquake many miles away,
and they came together urgently, not panicking.
They formed a circle, flank to flank, facing out,
ears opened out like wings, eyes scanning the horizon,
and in the center the youngest elephants, the most
    vulnerable,
protected.

The tremor passed, the elephants dispersed,
then quickly gathered one more time
when aftershocks shook them once again.

A circle of protection,
which they know innately how and when to cast.
They know, without argument,
when to gather, how to hold the ground, hold each other,
draw the circle wide.

So do we, friends, so do we.

Broken-Open Heartedness

REV. DR. SUSAN FREDERICK-GRAY

Living in the imperfect means welcoming what is undone—including the ways that we can become undone—and finding in this space a willingness to offer compassion to ourselves and others. A willingness to learn and grow. An ability to move through heartache, even shame, and try again.

In the midst of a world that breaks our heart again and again, I remember how our heartbreak is a direct result of our capacity for love and compassion. Our hearts break because we care. And when our hearts break, they also break open, reminding us of our profound interdependence. And by learning to make room for grief, our broken hearts become more capable of love and compassion, not less.

In this time of so much grief and tragedy, let our hearts break open wider and make space for more care and more humanity. And may this compassion guide our action and our commitment to a world of more love and justice.

Life Beyond Struggle

Rebeka Ndosi

Many of us—perhaps all of us—have experienced trauma. It can be difficult to heal from the wounds of our individual experiences and our environments.

Importantly, we have to ask ourselves why we want to heal. Is it for the cause? So we can put the armor back on and get back into the struggle? So we can continue to power through? In the social justice arena, how much you show that you are down for the cause, the amount of time you appear to spend visibly struggling, the day-to-day challenge that it can be to live as a person outside of nondominant culture, to live outside of whiteness, can be like a badge of honor. At a certain point, email signatures popped up everywhere: "Yours in the struggle."

But the badge of struggle is not the fullest expression of ourselves that we can be. As individuals, we must move beyond the narrative of only healing from trauma and tell a new story of ourselves, a story in which we intentionally dive deeply into our true identity as people who are and were always whole and ever interconnected.

Nor can we ever heal by accommodating ourselves to the culture of whiteness and white supremacy. Any social justice or liberation work is a struggle against these systems. After years of working in the nonprofit sector as a bridge builder, connector, and organizer for racial justice, I realized that I was smack dab in the middle of an economy that relied on our suffering and struggle. I perceived the vicious circle of working on behalf of folks who are and have been disenfranchised, yet all the while depending on the existence of their disenfranchisement for funding. Funding requirements often support initiatives that look and sound cool and make us feel good about ourselves but are not sustainable solutions. They tend not to allow for the time, depth, and commitment that lasting change requires. Those of us dedicated to creating change would have worked ourselves out of jobs if we lived in an empowerment economy.

I cannot help but look at struggle energetically. Two (or more) energetic things are going on in justice work.

In Soul Answer Healing, we call them trances. Trances are bodies of stuck energy that have taken on a life of their own. The stuckness is caused by harm, violence, and injury and disrupts energy flow. Over time, if not addressed and healed, trances grow bigger and bigger and become mistaken for how things are, no matter how painful they may be. There are the societal trances at the roots of the injustices we experience and work to end, and there are the individual trances we carry. Both types need healing, but little importance or value is ascribed to healing our personal traumas. We learn over time that our duty to the cause is to expend all our energy in combatting and putting a stop to (and sometimes healing, but not always) our deep societal trances while denying the need for any healing of our own.

What you focus on manifests and grows. When we focus on struggle, we get more of it. We continue to struggle when we focus on societal wounds and ignore our own. Is it any wonder that justice work is fraught with dysfunction and perpetuation of harm? The more we struggle to survive, the more we become exhausted, drained, and burned out when the struggle is not balanced by something to support our vitality and nourish our spirits.

The remedy to the harm done in focusing so much of our livelihoods on the struggle for justice is to reframe the truth of our wholeness. We are designed to heal and live into the fullness of our possibility and purpose. I offer us all light for our evolving and for who we are becoming.

PTSD Recovery and Reconciliation

Rev. Jami Yandle and Natalie Briscoe

is not pretty.
Focusing on what is
actually being said,
beyond the trickster lens
of a trauma response,
is not easy
does not feel good.

But courage lives in the stubbornness
we learned,
transformed into
the persistence
we need,
fueled by our
grit and sheer determination
to love ourselves
whole again.

When trauma tries
to trick us,
we can become
the Prankster,
turning it on
its head.

It says,
use these tools
to separate yourself
to protect yourself
to remain.

We say,
we will use these tools
to love ourselves
to learn ourselves
to move again.

Prayer for Transformation

Rev. Daniel Lawlor

Spirit of Life and Love,
bigger than the universe,
smaller than a grain of sand,
help us rebuild from the ruins of patriarchy and white supremacy.
Unpack the forces of repression in our hearts and institutions.
Let us imagine and work toward repair, healing and transformation.
May we remember the wider stories that our lives are a part of, seek humility,
and live into the healing we have encountered and are called to create.
Through the power of Love unfolding, Amen.

Prayer for Hope

Rev. Lindasusan V. Ulrich

Spirit of Hope . . .
            . . . help me.
I can't seem to find my way back to your realm.
I've been wandering in labyrinths
        fumbling in the darkness
        panicking at nearby growls
        losing count of left turns
Ariadne's thread only tangles my feet
and leaves my fingers raw.

Spirit of Hope . . .
            . . . ground me.
I've lost my bearings on what's real
        who I am
        how I got here
        why it matters
Unreality makes a poor compass.
I remember to look up

lest I get caught off-guard,
but such preparation means little
to a soul suffering vertigo.

Spirit of Hope . . .
            . . . steady me.
Maybe my only way forward is to stay still.
Perhaps if I rest my bones exactly where I am,
      instead of scrabbling for purchase
      searching for loopholes
      willing myself on
the dust will settle enough for a path to reappear.
It needn't be tended and beautiful—just discernible.

Spirit of Hope . . .
            . . . guide me.
You dwell in the turnaround between exhale and inhale—
a moment of trust that pulls me into the future.
I've been looking for something
      more grand
      more obvious
      more compelling
not recognizing the promise in the flickering signs:
my body already knows the way home.

Prayer for Living in Tension

Rev. Joseph M. Cherry, *Voices from the Margins*

If we have any hope of transforming the world and
changing ourselves,
We must be
bold enough to step into our discomfort,
brave enough to be clumsy there,
loving enough to forgive ourselves and others.

May we, as a people of faith, be granted the strength
to be
so bold,
so brave,
and so loving.

Be Her Cheerleader

Evan McGinness

When I was a teenager, my younger sister, Katie, was diagnosed with a deadly combination of illnesses, anorexia nervosa and Graves' disease. The first is a mental illness and the latter an autoimmune disease, both of which present with uncontrolled weight loss as their primary symptom.

It might seem impossible for someone to willingly starve themselves after getting diagnosed with a disease that causes severe weight loss. However, in therapy, Katie and I realized that we had matching dysfunctional mindsets: "When I am in control, I hope. When things are out of my control, I despair." For example, Katie may have believed that if she was going to experience starvation, it should be by her own hand rather than against her will. In order to heal, we first had to untangle this dysfunctional belief system.

When our family therapist told me to "Be her cheerleader, not her parent," I was offended. Naturally, I had assumed that the plan to prevent my sister from dying would include giving me multiple responsibilities regarding her care. But my immediate sensation of offense came from a deeper conflict. I felt that my parents were incompetent and that asking them to pay careful attention to my sister would be a death sentence. I had been Katie's "parent" all her life, and I was not going to give up my role at a time when she needed me the most! Eventually, I came to realize that my self-parentification was enabling my parents' passivity. Why would they need to perform any emotional labor when I was already doing it for them?

I eventually came around to the idea of being a cheerleader. I told myself that I would temporarily try it and monitor the outcome. I relinquished my iron grip and . . . it was fine! Giving my parents back their own roles and responsibilities gave me the space to change. The rational, analytical problem-solver transformed into a compassionate, optimistic cheerleader.

Ultimately, Katie needed me to be a wellspring of hope that she could drink from, not a robotic life manager. A journal entry I had written during this time has always stuck with me: "If you have to check 'love thy neighbor as thyself' off a to-do list, the living loving-kindness of your actions has already died."

I believe that hope flourishes in the darkest of times; it is more like a mushroom than an orchid. Mushrooms love damp soil, rotting wood, and dung heaps. Orchids require extensive control over their light levels, watering, humidity, and temperature. Hope is not cultivated in a greenhouse by a seasoned florist; it springs forth naturally from despair and decay.

Too often, we choose the route of the florist. We assume that by taking full control, we can solve our loved one's problems. Allow hope to arise from despair and let it nourish you. When you are replenished, be someone's cheerleader.

Eight and a Half Minutes

Rev. Kelly Weisman Asprooth-Jackson

93 million miles. That is the rough average distance that the light from the nearest star—our sun—must cover to reach the Earth. 93 million miles that light has to travel to make the conditions for life possible here. To allow a world on which trees can blossom, and rain can fall, and you and I may live. And the trip it takes across the gulf of space to reach us lasts about eight and a half minutes.

93 million miles seems like an impossible distance to beings such as ourselves, with bodies that are infinitely heavier than light and dramatically slower. But eight and a half minutes is a unit of measure we ourselves can make use of. It is time enough to break a heart with carelessness or cruelty, to ruin someone's week or shatter someone's dreams. And it is also long enough to write an email to an old friend or to lose a game of checkers to your young child. In that time, you could sing three songs, walk down the hall and introduce yourself to

your neighbors in the next apartment, or call up your brother and tell him you're sorry.

Eight and a half minutes might not be enough time to say everything we want to say, but it is enough to start the conversation. It might not be enough to do everything we want to do, but it is long enough to begin to do what we must. With the same seconds it takes for the sun's light to reach us, we can give the world, or some small piece of it, a new chance to flourish and grow.

In every moment, day and night, light from the sun touches somewhere on the earth. Our world depends on this—we could not be here without it. Nor could we be here without the moments of kindness and mercy on which our world also depends.

Meeting the Divine

Rev. Summer Albayati

I know you are tired
I am too
I know you are scared
How can you not be?
This time has brought us such tumult,
such babel.
I don't know about you,
but I find such confusion as I sift through
the sands of daily living
in search of the golden nuggets of wisdom.
But what if we were to leave our searching for the divine?
And not attempt to build a tower
nor to reach up to the heavens
searching for the right words to describe our feelings,
as imperfect as they may be,
but look into the eyes of our loved ones before us
reach across our borders
and open our gates.

Cross the seas
and give ourselves over
to the rocking of its waves.
Close our eyes and
breathe in the salty air
one breath at a time.
What if we were to stop the worry
and listen for those moments that
speak the religion of love
upon our tongues
over and over?
What if that would be the instant we met
one of the ninety-nine attributes of God?
Compassionate, Merciful, Restorer, Justice
Truth, Patience, Kindness, Wisdom
Loving, Forgiving, Peace . . . Oneness
And what if that was the point all along?
It's not about being perfect
It's not about running the perfect meeting or worship service
It's not about pleasing everyone.
It's okay if we fail
It's okay if we mess up

What if perfection was not the point
but meeting the divine each moment of our existence?
What would that mean for all that you've experienced?
What choices would you make now?

Don't Believe Your Own Press Release

AISHA HAUSER

One of the most valuable lessons I've learned in my career, especially as a faith leader, is to not believe my own press release. A press release typically presents a sanitized, surface-level perspective—all of the good and none of the bad, or the simply more complicated.

As a faith leader, it is sometimes intoxicating to have many people, mostly strangers, applaud your work and presence. Most people thrive on praise and accolades, and I am no exception. The flip side of this, of course, is that people will also project their fears, insecurities, and pain onto leaders. It is relatively easy for me to navigate the negativity and keep it at arm's length. While still at times painful, I am able to contextualize the source of negative projections.

It has been more difficult to learn how to contextualize the positive projections of people who do not know me personally. While I absolutely appreciate praise from groups of people I'll never meet, the fact is that even praise and love from afar is still projection. People project their hopes, dreams, and needs onto faith leaders. You may think that this is positive, and in many ways it is. But when a leader makes a mistake and falls from grace, those same people who showered them with adoration can just as quickly turn and go on the attack.

I have surrounded myself with a small circle of mentors, friends, and colleagues who I know will tell me the truth, even and especially when it is difficult. This gives me an opportunity to reflect on how I show up in the world, how I am perceived, and whether that matches how I see myself. I have tried very hard to avoid experiencing myself as a savior. As a UU, I don't believe in any savior, and I don't want to ever think I will become one myself.

No one person can save another who doesn't want to be saved. What we can do is strengthen our sense of self through relationship. We can learn to love and be loved, to care for each other and move through the challenges of life with others. When we learn to trust those around us who know us and value who we are, we can trust they will tell us the harder truths in love.

Next

NATALIE BRISCOE

What do we do now?
What's next?
We go looking for what
makes us feel
good.
Not distracted, not dazed,
not asleep, not anesthetized.
We find what makes us whole,
centered, grounded, and at peace.
It's okay not to know
right away.
Looking may not even
be all that fun.
It might be unsettling,
or even lonely.
But keep moving toward it.
Wait for it to arrive
like a deer in the forest.

Cultivating a life such as this
peace in the midst of pain,
progress after permanent injury—
takes practice
and patience.
It's okay to be afraid
or embarrassed.
But one thing this metamorphosis
does not require
is shame.

In faith, and hope,
and the greatest love there is,
we will find the *we* that
gets to good.
It is astounding,
the resilience of our own souls,
Especially when they are
joined together in
the co-creation
of the next.

Compassion

Linnea Nelson

Sometimes it's easier to love globally than locally.

When a hurricane hits or earthquakes erupt, our compassion runs deep for those left homeless or hurt. Yet when a member of our community becomes passive-aggressive, argumentative, or just can't hear that there might be another way to do things, our compassion can seem unreachable.

When gun violence erupts, when human rights are taken away, and when people are shamed for being who they are, our compassion re-emerges and runs deep. Yet when someone doesn't like a particular worship service or way that you do your work, and they feel completely at ease telling you that you are wrong, misguided, or unworthy, our compassion can dissipate quite quickly.

When our democracy is at risk and climate change looms, our compassion for the world, and all who live in it, runs deep. Yet, no matter how many kudos are given for the work that we do, one comment can derail us for a day a week or a month. And we can sometimes conjure compassion for the speaker but not for ourselves.

And where does this compassion arise to do our multifaceted, demanding, unforgiving work in this world? From the compassion we give to ourselves.

Let compassion fill our souls to remind us that we are worthy. We are guided by the spirit. And we are sometimes wrong, but more often we are simply engaging deeply in this messy, challenging work of feeding souls and transforming ourselves and the world.

Compassion.

For the world.

For those we hold close.

For ourselves.

Our Fear and Our Courage

Rev. Dr. Natalie Fenimore

> "Courage is resistance to fear, mastery of fear, not absence of fear."
>
> —Mark Twain

Courage is the ability to do something that frightens you. It is not actually having no fear at all.

Can we ever really approach a task without any fear at all? Each of has known failure and disappointment, hurt and sorrow. It is the way of being alive and human to know these are always possibilities. And doesn't that then predispose us to fear?

In many circumstances, fear is not unreasonable. Physical and emotional hurt are real in our lives. There is illness—including Covid-19—and violence, and climate disasters ravish communities around the world. We learn to fear the storm after seeing the damage and know that it makes sense to evacuate, to get out of the way, when it looks like it might happen again. Staying is a gamble, and we might only stay in the way of the storm if circumstances make it impossible to leave.

To move through life as if it is impossible for you to be hurt is not courageous—it is foolhardy. No one is in complete control of every situation. But even when the world is dangerous, I do believe that there is courage in moving forward anyway.

To have courage is to face danger and meet it with resolve, with bravery, with commitment. It is being willing to step into hard places and do hard things.

To be courageous is to move past your fears. To move through and around and beyond them, finding ways to align your actions with your highest values and goals.

Some of our most courageous and prophetic people were just regular people before they did their "big thing." So very much like you, really. And when you are courageous, you can inspire others to be so in turn.

It is also courageous—and can be deeply challenging—to look within yourself. Do you have the courage to be seen and known?

Our current times can bring us as leaders into ever deeper relationship with some of our deepest fears. We fear the knowledge that we are fallible and fragile and alone. We fear that we are capable of great wrong. And we fear that we cannot hide this from our God or our community or our own true hearts.

We must also reckon with the times we have not been humble or careful with the feelings of others. At some point we have all failed to live up to our best intentions. We may be afraid that we won't ever live up to our best intentions.

But we can also acknowledge our fears and act courageously. You can forgive and be forgiven. You can renew and recommit and turn again to a life lived with courage—the courage that comes from acting for the good. The courage that comes from a very real look into our own hearts.

We are not automatically condemned by any one past action. We can be forgiven for the hurt we have caused and for the times we have failed to act. We can renew ourselves and our resolve.

As people of faith, it may help to find a ritual or example that can bring you to this place of personal courage. Is there something that can help you recognize that you are brave enough to look into your own heart and see the beauty and love within you?

In community, we worship and learn and fellowship together to build our inner courage. We stand together for positive social change. Our spirits are refreshed by the landscape, the woods and gardens. We are a people of hope engaging with our connectedness.

There is so much courage among and within us, and this community is a place to live in the most courageous ways. May it be so.

Brave Enough for Goodness

Rev. Sean Parker Dennison

Spirit of Life, train our minds and our hearts to seek goodness. We are so constantly being trained in skepticism, disbelief, and doubt. Everywhere we go we hear that the end is near. And it may be—but even so, we must not be convinced that the only thing there is to do is give up.

Yes, the earth is endangered. Yes, we are bearing witness to people doing terrible things. Yes, even in our community, our faith, our families there is discord, disagreement, and disrespect. We see it and we feel it. Anxiety has taken root among us. It is hard to trust, hard to find our stores of generosity when so much is at stake.

But we know—oh, please let us know—that the only way to save the world is to believe in its goodness: to believe in the sweet air, free of the smoke and ash of fires burning; to believe in healthy waters pulsing through streams and rivers into the vast and sparkling oceans that give life again and again and again; to believe in the nourishing earth, fertile and unspoiled, holding tendrils and trees with her dark, tender hands; to believe in ecosystems and communities, cities, and nations that exist to help all beings thrive, governments that care for the people and for all that sustains us.

Cynicism and despair are not noble. They are not signs of intellect or proof of wisdom. It is never wise to give up. It is never wise to argue against hope, against goodness, against Life.

Courageous Love, help us be brave enough to believe in goodness, imagining, and thus creating the possibility of a happy ending, even though this part of the human story looks dire and the forces of evil and hatred seem strong. Let us imagine and then do whatever we can to increase the odds of goodness. Let us do this, most of all, by doing and being good.

Amen. Asé. Blessed Be.

We Dream of Peace

Rev. Marta I. Valentín, *Voices from the Margins*

Loving Spirit
of this and every sacred moment,
be with us in times of self-doubt
when we forget that dreams are not born in an instant
but must be nurtured,
must be chosen over and over.
When the world is telling us that we are dreaming too large,
too wild, too unrealistic, or even
too small,
remind us, gentle, patient Spirit,
that any dream worth waiting for
is worth working toward.

Precious and Loving God,
today more than ever
we dream of peace—
peace in our hearts, which have been

clouded over with promises
of a free world
that will never come to pass
if bought with the blood of war.

Dear God, today we dream of peace . . .
today we dream of peace.

Rest Is Crucial

Rev. Dr. Susan Frederick-Gray

> "I am one soft animal among many; a cell in the breathing world's body. Let us be cared for as such."
>
> —Atena O. Danner, *Incantations for Rest*

What times we are living through. We are in the churn of change. Systems and practices we've relied on are breaking down, and what is needed is still being imagined, not yet here.

When we are worn down and worn out, sometimes we still push ourselves, knowing the urgency and importance of the challenges ahead. But to bring forth the creativity, energy, and compassion needed to nurture change, we need to take care of ourselves.

Rest is crucial for the quality and sustainability of our bodies, our spirits, and our leadership. It is the seedbed of imagination, generosity, and inspiration. In this busy season, give yourself permission to tend to the soft care of your body and spirit.

There remains much work ahead. I have faith we will find ourselves renewed by taking time for play, for naps, for gardening, for stargazing, for what brings us joy and peace. This time will remind us of our wholeness as human beings; it will connect us to our joy as a source of resilience for our spirit.

Spirit of Life, in the midst of challenge and change, may we cultivate moments of being showered in blessings and held in the arms of joy and peace.

Thanksgiving for a Successful Workday

Pastor Joshua Berg

The day is done.
I'm so tired

Of laundry and dishes
while feeling always unclean

Of things constantly breaking
while feeling myself broken

Of desperately needing
while being needed

Of incessant anxiety
with pretense that all will be well

Of pain, physical and emotional,
While striving for a little physical fitness

Of relentlessly

seeking
fearing
wishing
toiling
while wanting just to sleep.

I'm so tired
of being tired!

I am grateful for rest.

The Church Where Everything Goes Wrong

Rev. Elea Kemler, *How We Are Called*

Six weeks into the church year, I have realized that I am the minister of a church where things usually go wrong. This morning the copy machine jams repeatedly. The bulletin describing the order of worship has been copied with the second page first and also upside down. No one has remembered to turn on the lights in the sanctuary before the service, so it is dark because it is raining outside. The microphone is buzzing and lets out a painful, high-pitched squeal, which makes people wince. We have just started the service when someone runs up with a bunch of flowers for the altar, just as someone else runs in with the silk arrangements we keep for the mornings when no one brings real flowers. There is laughter as the two flower bearers meet at the altar. They decide on the real flowers, and things settle down for a little while until a baby starts crying, which sets off another baby crying. I try to speak over the wailing as their fathers hustle them down the aisle and try to distract them in the back. Usually, I love watching the tall, gentle fathers who bounce their babies in backpacks at the rear of the sanctuary, but today I am annoyed because I want it to be quiet and holy and lovely and things are definitely not shaping up that way.

The woman who is helping with worship gets up and, instead of giving the announcements, introduces the candle-lighting time, which comes later. People call out, "Not yet!" More laughter. The organist starts playing the wrong hymn and a couple of choir members yell over the din for him to stop; a few minutes later, during the period for prayerful silence, he accidentally falls onto the keyboard, causing the organ to emit horrible, gassy noises. Shrieks and snorts of laughter. All pretense of Sunday morning decorum is lost and something inside me, some furious, bossy desire to have "my worship service" go according to my plan, finally slides free and I can laugh with them.

This will be the first of many times that I laugh at Sunday morning details gone awry. It is also the first of many times that I imagine God is watching, looking up or down or over at us from wherever God sits on Sunday mornings, slightly amazed and maybe at a loss for words because we, God's people, are so funny and wonderful and odd all at the same time. In moments like these I imagine God as a sturdy old woman with her hands on her hips, or perhaps as a rabbi pulling on his long, white beard. I imagine a God shaking his head and saying, "What in the world are they doing over there? This is what they call church? What were they thinking?"

But I also imagine a God who is touched and maybe a little honored by our efforts, however halting, to worship and give praise. I imagine a God who is moved by our attempts to care for one another and to name things we know as holy. There is a warmth in this congregation that is new to me, a simple friendliness that shines through the fumblings and failures, a love that makes the ragged edges smooth. I have always wanted to believe that kindness and compassion matter more than anything. I sense that we can learn this here.

Go Deeper

Rev. Jim Rigby

While we each express something unique and important about the universe, it is also true that there are no free agents in the web of life. Nature does not consist of individuals so much as ecologies.

When we feel lost or alone, there is always peace to be found by going deeper into what we share with others.

Let the salt in your tears remind you of your mother, the ocean.

Let the red blood in your veins be a reminder you were also forged from iron in faraway stars.

Let the oxygen in your lungs be a reminder you are not an island but are interwoven with every plant and animal in one intimate body of mutual breathing.

Let the mathematics in your head remind you of your home in the silent and invisible patterns that lay behind the visible cosmos.

When facing loss and despair, peace is always to be found by going deeper. Alone, each of us seems a mere vapor, but we are tasting a deeper immortality every time we love.

Paddling, No Water

Rev. Meg Barnhouse, *Did I Say That Out Loud?*

I have learned some things about life from canoes. I'm not saying I know how to paddle. I have been in canoes twice, and both have been learning experiences. The second time was fun.

The first time, a friend and I decided to take one out on a lake. We slid the canoe into the water. She hopped in. I put one foot on the ladder from the dock and one foot into the canoe, holding on to the dock like a sensible person. The canoe tipped over, threw her out, filled with water, and sank to the bottom, about four feet under the water. She pulled herself back up onto the dock, dripping. I was still hanging on to the ladder.

From this I learn that there are some situations in life where it is dumb to be cautious. You just have to let go, put your whole self in instead of hedging your bets. The trick is to figure out when you are in such a situation, because often it's smart to be cautious.

I took hold of the rope at the front of the canoe, still attached to the dock, and heaved the thing up out of the water. The canoe was heavy, and I was in my mid-forties at the time. Did I ask for help? No. Did I get the canoe back up onto the deck? Yes, in one heave. Did I hurt myself? You bet. Torn rotator cuff. It's gotten lots better, but I use the twinges it still gives me to remind myself to ask for help.

The next time—the fun time—I was on the river in Virginia at a canoe workshop, where the whole purpose was to teach people how to paddle. Nothing but my pride got hurt this time.

Here is what happened. The river was low because of a drought that year. Quite low.

We put in at a bend where the river was deep enough for us to paddle around in pairs. I got instructions on the proper way to get into a canoe, the motion of the paddle, the knack of coordinating with my paddling partner, the rhythm and glide.

For a couple of hours we paddled in pairs, and then it was time for solo work. By this time we were downriver a bit. The instructors sat in one canoe. They paddled fast down a stretch of river and then turned sideways to us so they could help us by shouting suggestions. I didn't know where the others were (back up the river, I think), but I was trying to get to where the instructors were. The water was so shallow that I couldn't get much pressure with the paddle; it kept slipping through the water or knocking against the rocks on the bottom. "Try paddling faster," they shouted. I stepped it up. The canoe moved maybe a foot forward.

I come from a culture that believes in trying hard. I was taught that success is 10 percent inspiration and 90 percent perspiration. And it's true, of course. Except when it's not. I paddled, fast and furious, on that drought-stricken stretch of river, until I noticed the instructors laughing.

"You can get out and just walk it down here to where the water's deeper," they shouted.

Oh.

Sometimes we try too hard or in the wrong way. We push too hard, poke at things too much, take on things that aren't ours, take over when we're not supposed to. I'm going to plan, in my life, not to try so hard in water that's too shallow. I have asked my inner wisdom to throw that picture up on the inner screen when I'm in that kind of situation—working the paddles through that inch and a half of water, hearing the divine instructors, the angel guides, up ahead just guffawing. Yeah, that'll help.

Rest

Rev. Eileen Casey-Campbell

I don't know
Who lied to you
But you don't have
To earn your rest
Morsel by meager
Morsel with an
Unrelenting stream of
Labors. You are
Good. Whole. Worthy
Of this sabbath,
Payment withstanding.
Every moment of
Delicious repose you
Savor is free
Of charge.
It is your being

Not your doing
That grants you
Holy respite.

We all know
Who lied to you
And the only antidote
Is to be utterly
Useless for a time.
So rest here
Awhile. Lay your body
And your burdens down.
Be still and know
Your every blissful,
Quiet breath is
A prayer of gratitude
For abundant grace:
Thank you. I have
All that I need. And
So I rest.

One Gregarious Reindeer

Cameron Young

My parents always said I was born for the stage. While I have since formally trained as a singer and an actor, one of my favorite moments on a stage was also my first time. My preschool class was performing "Rudolph the Red-Nosed Reindeer" at our school's Christmas pageant, and my eagerness for the moment was unparalleled. We were all dressed up as little Rudolphs—paper antlers, brown turtlenecks, and noses red from Crayola washable markers. However, I was stunned to find out we would actually be singing *in front of* the stage! The kids five and up got to be on stage, but the younger ones had been relegated down below. I'm not sure if it was for liability reasons or if they feared we would suffer from stage fright (not me).

On the verge of a tantrum, I reluctantly began singing. I peeked at the stage behind me and felt it beckoning. Then and there, I decided not to let my opportunity to shine pass me up. I willfully climbed up on the large stage and began belting. As if that wasn't extra enough, I started shredding on air guitar. My friend even decided to get in the action and climb on stage too, accompanied by the roaring sounds of parents' laughter and the mortified look on my teacher's face.

You might be familiar with Abraham Maslow's hierarchy of needs, which states that the beginning stages of life are born in self-preservation and many become self-actualized as adults. What many don't know is that Maslow borrowed these concepts from time he spent with people of the Blackfoot Nations, who he found to be more cooperative, egalitarian, and self-confident than the people he knew back home. However, he fundamentally *got it wrong*. Not only was self-actualization only the beginning step, with the final stage being community actualization or cultural perpetuity, but the Blackfoot and many other indigenous tribes hold that individuals are actually born self-actualized. My grandmother, who is of Cherokee descent, used to say, "Kids are perfect until they become civilized." Buddhists might even call this beginner's mind.

Think about the absolute perfection of a newborn baby. As that child grows, they become constrained by social conventions, experience inevitable trauma, and feel their self-preservation threatened. Only then does that child develop the propensity to really harm others and themselves. That's where community comes in—a community that can love and protect that child can ensure they remain self-actualized.

Whenever I am feeling paralyzed by anxiety or indecision, I try to remember that gregarious reindeer and tap into my inner child. The kid with reckless abandon who lacked awareness about social rules and had a healthy disregard for authority. The kid who simply wanted to sing and be heard. The kid who was born for the stage. May we all find those literal and metaphorical stages that have beckoned to us since childhood. May we all know we're perfect, just as we are.

God's Work

Rev. Elizabeth Tarbox, *Life Tides*

What is God's work? If God is immanent and transcendent, in and out of everything, then how could it be possible not to do God's work? Surely all work is God's work—there is nothing which is not of God. Is there?

But that doesn't do it, somehow. There are times when what I do is strictly for me. God or no God, I'm working for myself, even during those times when God would probably approve. Mostly what I do for myself is compatible with what I believe I would do for God.

But not always. There are times of conflict, when the prompting and urging of my desire are up against the sentinel of my conscience. They square off, these two strong voices somewhere deep in the thick of me where there is no judge, no referee, and mercifully no spectators. "Do it," say I. "Don't," says God. One of them wins and the other goes grumbling away, threatening and complaining in the basement of my being like a boiler with an excess of steam. And I am left to live with my decision, to forgive or applaud, to bask in my nobility or blush in my shame. And God and I make peace once more.

Then there are times when I can't tell which is God's voice and which is my own. What about those times when God seems to be saying "Do it" and I am saying "No." When God says, "This is the right thing to do," and I, shaking with fear, confess, "I can't, I'm just too scared."

"I'll be with you."
"How do I know?"
"You can do it, be not afraid."
"I might fail, make a fool of myself."
"Yes you might. Do it anyway."
"But people might not like me."
"That's right."
"But how do I know this is good? How can I be sure?"
"You cannot be sure. This is a risk."

Yes, those are the toughest times: wanting to do right without losing my safety, not knowing if I am doing

God's work, or using God to do mine. There is no superhighway named Right Way. There are no signposts, no guides, no promises, no guarantees; only the lonely voice of conscience and the cringing cry of fear wrestling each other in inner space. Those are the times of lying awake at night and staring at the detail of the day through a haze of worry, working and reworking the "oughts," the "should," and "yes, buts" of the thing.

And what's to be done, but to listen to the voice that seems to be speaking a consistent truth, move through the fear to trust the moral judgements we have lived by, and pray for courage.

From *Radical Hospitality: Benedict's Way of Love*

LONNI COLLINS PRATT AND FATHER DANIEL HORMAN

Everything matters.
You are not alone.
You are more than you know.
The awful thing is not the final word.
Today is all we have and today is enough.
We need each other.

There Are No Right Words

Rev. JeKaren Bell

When your heart has crumbled
No healing balm
Can fix
Or patch
Each and every crack
Making the pain
Invisible
And unfelt

No
There are no words that can change time
To make things light
And easy
And forgettable
Erased

But there are words
When drawn from deep within
That can be a container

For hurts that sink deep
Unspoken
Words that give scaffolding
To bits and pieces that are tempted
To fall.

You Are Not on Call

Liz James

you are not on call
for the pain of the world
I know you feel every hit of the hammer,
beating plowshares into swords,
and people into plowshares
and every time you fail to step between
the blow and its target
the injustice is sewn into your bones too

and so
when the hammer rises, you must rise with it
raising your voice, your eyes, your awareness, your body
whatever part of you that can be given as an offering

you cannot stay this way forever,
sewn to this cacophony of blows
every movement of yours a following
until your body is owned by the drumbeat of
the raising of weapons

until your days string together in a stuttering
heartbreak of rage
and you cannot
catch
breath

but this is what you promised
to those who don't get to choose whether or to show
up for the fight
to those whose very bodies thrust them into the ring
you promised
that you would hold nothing back
I know

except—you cannot be on call
for the pain of the world
it is not work that can be done
without sleep

when we said that people are too sacred to be
beaten into plowshares
or swords
we meant you

we need you
for the fight
and we need you for all the things
that are less, and more, than fighting

we need you to be ready to listen in the soft way earth listens
to rain in the hours before dawn
to be tender, to cradle precious things, to hold the smell of dew in your hair
to hum the song that flowers
will rise up through the earth to hear

I need you
to stay
in love with the world

Hope

Rosemerry Wahtola Trommer, *All the Honey*

Hope has holes
in its pockets.
It leaves little
crumb trails
so that we,
when anxious,
can follow it.
Hope's secret:
it doesn't know
the destination—
it knows only
that all roads
begin with one
foot in front
of the other.

A Blessing for Those Who Bless

Linnea Nelson

May today open you to at least one of these blessings:

A single blade of dewy grass
A leafy tree that feeds your soul
Soaring birds, fleeting dragonflies
        Cats pawing for attention

Coffee to warm and invigorate
        from a very large mug
A hand-painted card
and note of appreciation
A meeting of holy aspirations
        and witnessing justice unfolding

Only one complaint
        that touches a nerve
An opportunity to create sacred space
        for the worried, the grieving,
        the overwhelmed, the angry

A creative endeavor
    meant only for your own pleasure
The completion of a task
    that will bring joy, organization, or deep meaning

An exchange filled with gratitude

A splash of wonder

A moment of awe

And, in a day when none of these appear,
May you be blessed by knowing that
You are held by a
Divine and abiding love
Each and every moment
Of every single day.

One Love

Rev. Dr. Hope Johnson, *Voices from the Margins*

We are one,
A diverse group
Of proudly kindred spirits
Here, not by coincidence—
But because we choose to journey—together.

We are active and proactive
We care, deeply
We live our love, as best we can.

We ARE one
Working, Eating, Laughing,
Playing, Singing, Storytelling, Sharing and Rejoicing.
Getting to know each other.
Taking risks
Opening up.
Questioning, Seeking, Searching . . .
Trying to understand . . .
Struggling . . .

Making mistakes
Paying Attention . . .
Asking Questions
Listening . . .
Living our Answers
Learning to love our neighbors
Learning to love ourselves.

Apologizing and forgiving with humility
Being forgiven, through Grace.

Creating the Beloved Community—Together
We are ONE.

A Prayer for Discernment

Rev. Tandi Rogers

Spirit of wisdom,
meet me in the still places
where the noise of obligation softens
and I can hear what is true.

Help me listen beneath urgency,
beyond fear,
past the voices that say I must stay
to prove my worth or my love.

If it is time to continue,
give me renewed clarity and courage.
If it is time to release,
give me the grace to loosen my grip
before resentment takes root.

Teach me the difference
between fatigue and calling,
between loyalty and fear,
between faithfulness and refusal to change.

Let me trust that I am not
the sole carrier of this work,
that what is meant to endure
does not depend on me alone.

Guide me toward the next faithful movement,
not the whole map,
not the perfect answer,
just enough light
for today.
Amen.

After

Rev. Summer Albayati

After the march
After the turning and churning of the storm
After the bodies are laid to rest
the ashes twirling in the sky
scattered across the land
allowing their memories to bless us with more hope
After the pains of birthing
A new way of thinking, feeling, articulating
something we know deep within our hearts
to be the call of the Divine
toward more love, more justice, more equity

After all that, we gaze towards the sky
witnessing the majesty of the universe
The compassion and mercy of a divine spark
And we dream some more
as our thoughts rise up to the shimmering lights
showering us with rays of new possibilities

of love made real
on the ground—right here

After the rest
After resting in these moments of renewal
sent to us by a force of love that turns the earth
over and over again
we can become reborn, renewed
And then we can remember that
the healing begins when we
reach out
into the unknown
Breathing into each moment
of new possibilities
The healing begins
when we rest in the knowledge
that there are others reaching toward us too